WALKING WITH JESUS IN NEW LIFE

A 30-Day Easter Journal

Friendship Press®

Friendship Press
P.O. Box 117
Wyncote, PA 19095

Library of Congress Catalog-in-Publication data available upon request

ISBN (hardcover): 978-1-961088-12-2

Verse selection and prompts by Courtney Richards
Cover and interior design by Laurie Ingram

Typesetting by Integra Software Services Pvt. Ltd.
Printed in the United States of America

About This Journal

Easter isn't (just) a Sunday. Easter is a season. Easter Sunday is obviously an important day, a cornerstone of the Christian faith and worship life, when the faithful not only mark but relive the wonder of the resurrection of Jesus Christ. But Easter Sunday isn't the day that a holy season (Lent) ends – it is the day that a whole new season begins. The season of *Easter* carries from Easter Sunday 'til the day of Pentecost, 50 days (not counting Sundays) of *walking with Jesus in new life*, making every effort to live into the promise of renewal and possibility.

This *30 Day Easter Journal* provides 30 prompts to move you through this season – not quite one a day, but more than enough to draw close to the Holy in this unique season. Thirty readings have been selected from across all three years of the Revised Common Lectionary cycle, representing the depth and breadth of our sacred scriptures – matched with thirty prompts encourage your reflection and response.

Perhaps this journal is something you'll use each day as a focused devotional time; or maybe you'll pick it up more occasionally and as time allows. There is space for you to add the date on each entry, and to write and respond in whatever way is meaningful. Maybe this is a personal devotion, or maybe you'll invite a trusted prayer partner or small group to read and reflect together.

However, whenever, and wherever you make use of this resource, we pray that you find the Living Word opened to you in a new way, and that renewed life, faith, and hope will find you – this Easter, and always.

date

JOHN 20:11-16

But Mary stood weeping outside the tomb. As she wept, she bent over to look into the tomb, and she saw two angels in white sitting where the body of Jesus had been lying, one at the head and the other at the feet. They said to her, "Woman, why are you weeping?" She said to them, "They have taken away my Lord, and I do not know where they have laid him." When she had said this, she turned around and saw Jesus standing there, but she did not know that it was Jesus. Jesus said to her, "Woman, why are you weeping? Whom are you looking for?" Supposing him to be the gardener, she said to him, "Sir, if you have carried him away, tell me where you have laid him, and I will take him away." Jesus said to her, "Mary!" She turned and said to him in Hebrew, "Rabbouni!" (which means Teacher).

date

She knew who he was when he called her by name. What about Jesus' story makes you feel most connected to him, most 'known'?

date

MARK 16:4-7

When they looked up, they saw that the stone, which was very large, had already been rolled back. As they entered the tomb, they saw a young man dressed in a white robe sitting on the right side, and they were alarmed. But he said to them, "Do not be alarmed; you are looking for Jesus of Nazareth, who was crucified. He has been raised; he is not here. Look, there is the place they laid him. But go, tell his disciples and Peter that he is going ahead of you to Galilee; there you will see him, just as he told you."

date

While they stand there being surprised, they are told to go and tell what they've seen. But do they even know yet? When have you known God was doing something in your life, but felt unable to explain or define it?

date

date

date

MARK 16:8

So they went out and fled from the tomb, for terror and amazement had seized them, and they said nothing to anyone, for they were afraid.

date

When has your fear held you back? What part of your faith – or what tactic, trick, or practice – allows you to carry on when you're afraid?

date

date

date

PSALM 118:1-2, 14, 17

O give thanks to the Lord, for he is good;
his steadfast love endures forever!
Let Israel say,
"His steadfast love endures forever." ...
The Lord is my strength and my might;
he has become my salvation. ...
I shall not die, but I shall live
and recount the deeds of the Lord.

date

What 'deeds' can you recount? When has God's goodness been so steadfast and evident you just had to share it?

date

PSALM 118:21-24

I thank you that you have answered me
  and have become my salvation.
The stone that the builders rejected
  has become the chief cornerstone.
This is the Lord's doing;
  it is marvelous in our eyes.
This is the day that the Lord has made;
  let us rejoice and be glad in it.

date

When have you felt rejected or cast aside? What brought you out of it – when did you realize you'd arrived at a place of gladness?

date

date

date

ISAIAH 25:6-8a

On this mountain the Lord of hosts will make for all peoples
a feast of rich food, a feast of well-aged wines,
of rich food filled with marrow, of well-aged wines strained clear.
And he will destroy on this mountain
the shroud that is cast over all peoples,
the covering that is spread over all nations;
he will swallow up death forever.

date

Consider a time you felt completely satisfied and filled with good things. What was it about that moment that had you feeling as if everything was in your favor?

date

date

date

ISAIAH 25:8b-9

Then the Lord God will wipe away the tears from all faces,
and the disgrace of his people he will take away from all the earth,
for the Lord has spoken.
It will be said on that day,
"See, this is our God; we have waited for him, so that he might save us.
This is the Lord for whom we have waited;
let us be glad and rejoice in his salvation."

date

Have you been waiting for something to change, be made right, or completed? How can you be part of the solution; what can you do while you're waiting for God's saving grace to be made known?

date

1 JOHN 1:1-3

We declare to you what was from the beginning, what we have heard, what we have seen with our eyes, what we have looked at and touched with our hands, concerning the word of life— this life was revealed, and we have seen it and testify to it and declare to you the eternal life that was with the Father and was revealed to us— what we have seen and heard we also declare to you so that you also may have fellowship with us, and truly our fellowship is with the Father and with his Son Jesus Christ.

date

How do your words and actions declare the life and fellowship you experience as a person of faith? What about your life would be different without this faith foundation?

date

date

date

JOHN 20:30-31

Now Jesus did many other signs in the presence of his disciples that are not written in this book. But these are written so that you may continue to believe that Jesus is the Messiah, the Son of God, and that through believing you may have life in his name.

date

'Many other signs.' What else would they need to see to know it was Jesus? When have you needed a sign to point out God's hand in something? How did you know it when it came?

date

date

date

REVELATION 5:11-12

Then I looked, and I heard the voice of many angels surrounding the throne and the living creatures and the elders; they numbered myriads of myriads and thousands of thousands, singing with full voice,

> "Worthy is the Lamb that was slaughtered
> to receive power and wealth and wisdom and might
> and honor and glory and blessing!"

date

Who do you count among your 'myriads and thousands'? Who has taught you to sing with full voice about the glory and blessing of the Holy?

date

PSALM 30:1-2, 11-12

You have turned my mourning into dancing;
you have taken off my sackcloth
and clothed me with joy,
so that my soul may praise you and not be silent.
O Lord my God, I will give thanks to you forever.

date

Recall a time you were relieved of a burden, when a grief was lifted. Give thanks for that season of ease and release; let your soul fully praise.

date

date

date

PSALM 4:7-8

You have put gladness in my heart
more than when their grain and wine abound.
I will both lie down and sleep in peace,
for you alone, O Lord, make me lie down in safety.

date

When are you most secure and at peace? What part does your faith or practice play in creating that calm and safety?

date

date

date

LUKE 24:28-32

As they came near the village to which they were going, he walked ahead as if he were going on. But they urged him strongly, saying, “Stay with us, because it is almost evening and the day is now nearly over.” So he went in to stay with them. When he was at the table with them, he took bread, blessed and broke it, and gave it to them. Then their eyes were opened, and they recognized him, and he vanished from their sight. They said to each other, “Were not our hearts burning within us while he was talking to us on the road, while he was opening the scriptures to us?”

date

They realized who Jesus was when he did the Jesus-y thing – took bread, blessed, broke, gave. How do others recognize Jesus in you? What do you intend/hope to be your calling card – how are things around you different because you know who Jesus is?

date

PSALM 23:1-3

The Lord is my shepherd; I shall not want.
He makes me lie down in green pastures;
he leads me beside still waters;
he restores my soul.
He leads me in right paths
for his name's sake.

date

What 'right path' is calling to you right now? Where does the Holy One need you to lead, or follow, or walk alongside?

date

date

date

1 JOHN 3:16-17

We know love by this, that he laid down his life for us—and we ought to lay down our lives for the brothers and sisters. How does God's love abide in anyone who has the world's goods and sees a brother or sister in need and yet refuses help?

date

How <u>does</u> God's love abide in one who refuses to help? Where have you held back, when you could have done more? Where do you find it easy to help – and when are you more reluctant?

date

date

date

JOHN 10:27-30

My sheep hear my voice. I know them, and they follow me. I give them eternal life, and they will never perish. No one will snatch them out of my hand. My Father, in regard to what he has given me, is greater than all, and no one can snatch them out of the Father's hand. The Father and I are one."

date

How do you tell the difference between the voice and call of the Holy Spirit, and the distractions and temptations of the world around you? When and where are you clearest and most engaged? How can you get yourself to that mental (or literal) place more often?

date

ACTS 8:29-31

Then the Spirit said to Philip, "Go over to this chariot and join it." So Philip ran up to it and heard him reading the prophet Isaiah. He asked, "Do you understand what you are reading?" He replied, "How can I, unless someone guides me?" And he invited Philip to get in and sit beside him.

date

Who is a good teacher in your faith life? Where do you look for insight and understanding? Who might be looking to you for the same thing – how can you serve as a mentor and guide?

date

date

date

REVELATION 21:1-4

Then I saw a new heaven and a new earth, for the first heaven and the first earth had passed away, and the sea was no more. And I saw the holy city, the new Jerusalem, coming down out of heaven from God, prepared as a bride adorned for her husband. And I heard a loud voice from the throne saying, "See, the home of God is among mortals.

He will dwell with them;
they will be his peoples,
and God himself will be with them and be their God;
he will wipe every tear from their eyes.
Death will be no more;
mourning and crying and pain will be no more,
for the first things have passed away."

date

What does the world around you – your part of the world, at least – look like when mourning and pain are gone, and God fully dwells among God's people? What part might you play in bringing that world into being?

date

date

date

PSALM 22:27-28

All the ends of the earth shall remember
  and turn to the Lord,
and all the families of the nations
  shall worship before him.
For dominion belongs to the Lord,
  and he rules over the nations.

date

What is 'dominion'? What does it mean for God to be 'over' everything? Does it leave you with nothing to do – or does it mean you have a bigger role – in how your world works?

date

PSALM 22:29-31

To him, indeed, shall all who sleep in the earth bow down;
before him shall bow all who go down to the dust,
and I shall live for him.
Posterity will serve him;
future generations will be told about the Lord
and proclaim his deliverance to a people yet unborn,
saying that he has done it.

date

How are you serving future generations – biological, professional, societal? What do you bring that others can learn – and what are you learning from those new and forming in the faith?

date

date

date

PSALM 148:9-12

Mountains and all hills,
  fruit trees and all cedars!
Wild animals and all cattle,
  creeping things and flying birds!
Kings of the earth and all peoples,
  princes and all rulers of the earth!
Young men and women alike,
  old and young together!

date

Imagine (or go to!) your favorite place to 'be in creation'. What is it about that place that resonates with the hum of Divine wonder? What makes that place special for you?

date

date

date

1 PETER 2:4-5

Come to him, a living stone, though rejected by mortals yet chosen and precious in God's sight, and like living stones let yourselves be built into a spiritual house, to be a holy priesthood, to offer spiritual sacrifices acceptable to God through Jesus Christ.

date

How is your 'spiritual house' these days? What areas are strong and resilient – and where could the house use some renovation and restoration? Where might you look for the support, supplies, and sustenance to make that renewal possible?

date

1 PETER 2:9-10

... But you are a chosen people, a royal priesthood, a holy nation, God's own people, in order that you may proclaim the excellence of him who called you out of darkness into his marvelous light. Once you were not a people, but now you are God's people; once you had not received mercy, but now you have received mercy.

date

What does it mean to receive mercy? What does that look and feel like in a real, everyday way? How can you show, offer, or be such mercy to another?

date

date

date

PSALM 98:3-4

He has remembered his steadfast love and faithfulness
  to the house of Israel.
All the ends of the earth have seen
  the victory of our God.
Make a joyful noise to the Lord, all the earth;
  break forth into joyous song and sing praises.

date

Think about (and listen to! or play!) a piece of music that brings your soul joy. What is it about this song that lifts you to a place of praise? (Maybe share it with someone who could use that same lift, telling them why it encourages and strengthens you.)

date

date

date

ACTS 1: 24-26

Then they prayed and said, “Lord, you know everyone’s heart. Show us which one of these two you have chosen to take the place in this ministry and apostleship from which Judas turned aside to go to his own place.” And they cast lots for them, and the lot fell on Matthias, and he was added to the eleven apostles.

date

How must it have felt to be the one chosen to sub in? (Matthias was 'voted in' as the 12th disciple, to take Judas's place after his betrayal of Jesus and his death.) How does a life of faith sometimes place you in an awkward spot, and how do you navigate your way through it?

date

PSALM 1:1-3

Happy are those
  who do not follow the advice of the wicked
or take the path that sinners tread
  or sit in the seat of scoffers,
but their delight is in the law of the Lord,
  and on his law they meditate day and night.
They are like trees
  planted by streams of water,
which yield their fruit in its season,
  and their leaves do not wither.
In all that they do, they prosper.

date

What sets you off, what makes you sit in that 'seat of scoffers'? How can you change your place, pulling yourself back to the trees planted by the streams, delighting in God's goodness, and staying close to the Holy's intention for you?

date

date

date

EZEKIEL 37:2-6

He led me all around them; there were very many lying in the valley, and they were very dry. He said to me, "Mortal, can these bones live?" I answered, "O Lord God, you know." Then he said to me, "Prophesy to these bones and say to them: O dry bones, hear the word of the Lord. Thus says the Lord God to these bones: I will cause breath to enter you, and you shall live. I will lay sinews on you and will cause flesh to come upon you and cover you with skin and put breath in you, and you shall live, and you shall know that I am the Lord."

date

What are you dreaming about these days? Where is God leading you to make connections? What can you build or rebuild for the good of your family, church, or community?

date

date

date

PSALM 97:11-12

Light dawns for the righteous
 and joy for the upright in heart.
Rejoice in the Lord, O you righteous,
 and give thanks to his holy name!

date

Pour out your gratitude today. Everything small and large, significant and ordinary – let that thanksgiving and goodness rise in you and overflow.

date

GENESIS 11:5-9

The Lord came down to see the city and the tower, which mortals had built. And the Lord said, "Look, they are one people, and they have all one language, and this is only the beginning of what they will do; nothing that they propose to do will now be impossible for them. Come, let us go down and confuse their language there, so that they will not understand one another's speech." So the Lord scattered them abroad from there over the face of all the earth, and they left off building the city. Therefore it was called Babel, because there the Lord confused the language of all the earth, and from there the Lord scattered them abroad over the face of all the earth.

date

When have you felt disconnected or misunderstood? How did you resolve that – how did you get someone to hear you clearly, or how did you learn to listen better to them?

date

date

date

ACTS 2:1-6

When the day of Pentecost had come, they were all together in one place. And suddenly from heaven there came a sound like the rush of a violent wind, and it filled the entire house where they were sitting. Divided tongues, as of fire, appeared among them, and a tongue rested on each of them. All of them were filled with the Holy Spirit and began to speak in other languages, as the Spirit gave them ability. Now there were devout Jews from every people under heaven living in Jerusalem. And at this sound the crowd gathered and was bewildered, because each one heard them speaking in the native language of each.

date

When have you felt most connected to community? What about that moment felt right, and even sacred? How can you create and nurture more moments of beloved community, for yourself and for others?

date

date

date